PHUKL...
A POCKET
TRAVEL GUIDE
2023

EXPLORE THE BEST OF PHUKET'S
ATTRACTIONS, BEACHES, AND HIDDEN
GEMS!
WITH THIS COMPREHENSIVE TRAVEL
GUIDE

DANIEL C. FLICK

Copyright©2023(Daniel c. Flick)

All intellectual property rights are retained. Without the express written permission of the publisher, no part of this book may be reproduced or transmitted in any form or by any means, electronic or mechanical, including photocopying, recording, or any information storing and retrieval system.

TABLE OF CONTENT

Phuket map

CHAPTER 1: WELCOME TO PHUKET

    1.1 About This Pocket Travel Guide

    1.2 How to use of This Guide

CHAPTER 2: GETTING TO KNOW PHUKET

    2.1 Phuket at a Glance

    2.2 History and Culture

    2.3 Local Customs and Etiquette

    2.4 Weather and Best Time to Visit

CHAPTER 3: TOP ATTRACTIONS IN PHUKET

    3.1 Old Phuket Town

    3.2 Big Buddha

    3.3 Wat Chalong

    3.4 Phang Nga Bay

    3.5 Phi Phi Islands

    3.6 Promthep Cape

    3.7 Kata Noi Beach

    3.8 Patong Beach

    3.9 Bangla Road

CHAPTER 4: OVERVIEW OF PHUKET BEACHES

    4.1 Patong Beach

    4.2 Kata Beach

    4.3 Karon Beach

    4.4 Kamala Beach

    4.5 Surin Beach

    4.6 Nai Harn Beach

    4.7 Freedom Beach

    4.8 Mai Khao Beach

CHAPTER 5: EXPLORING PHUKET'S CULTURE

    5.1 Temples and Shrines

    5.2 Traditional Festivals and Events

    5.3 Local Cuisine and Street Food

    5.4 Night Markets and Shopping

    5.5 Thai Massage and Wellness

CHAPTER 6: OUTDOOR ACTIVITIES IN PHUKET

    6.1 Island Hopping and Snorkeling

    6.2 Scuba Diving and Underwater Exploration

    6.3 Surfing and Watersports

    6.4 Hiking and Nature Trails

    6.5 Elephant Sanctuaries and Wildlife Reserves

CHAPTER 7: NIGHTLIFE AND ENTERTAINMENT

    7.1 Bangla Road

    7.2 Nightclubs and Bars

    7.3 Cabaret Shows and Ladyboy Performances

7.4 Beach Parties and Fire Shows

7.5 Live Music and Cultural Performances

CHAPTER 8: PRACTICAL INFORMATION

8.1 Transportation in Phuket

8.2 Accommodation Options

8.3 Dining and Cuisine

8.4 Money and Currency Exchange

8.5 Safety Tips and Emergency Contacts

Emergency Contacts:

CHAPTER 9: OFF THE BEATEN PATH

9.1 Secret Beaches and Hidden Coves

9.2 Authentic Local Experiences

9.3 Day Trips from Phuket

9.4 Eco-Tourism and Sustainable Initiatives

9.5 Exploring Nearby Islands and National Parks

CHAPTER 10: CONCLUSION

10.1 Phuket: Your Unforgettable Experience

10.2 Travel Resources and Additional Information

Phuket map

CHAPTER 1: WELCOME TO

Once upon a time, nestled in the turquoise waters of the Andaman Sea, there was a tropical paradise called Phuket. This enchanting island, known for its pristine beaches, lush rainforests, and vibrant culture, welcomed travelers from around the world with open arms.

As the sun rose over the horizon, casting a golden glow upon the palm-fringed shores, a sense of tranquility filled the air. The gentle waves whispered tales of ancient seafarers who once sailed these waters, leaving behind a legacy of adventure and discovery.

The story of Phuket unfolded as visitors stepped onto its sandy shores, ready to embark on their own extraordinary journeys. The island's rich history came to life in the streets of Old Phuket Town, where colonial architecture and vibrant colors painted a picture of days gone by. Temples and shrines whispered ancient prayers, offering a glimpse into the spiritual heart of the island.

But Phuket was not just a place of the past; it was a vibrant tapestry of cultures and traditions that thrived in harmony. Local markets bustled with activity, enticing visitors with exotic fruits, fragrant spices, and colorful textiles. The aroma of sizzling street food filled the air, inviting all to indulge in the tantalizing flavors of Thai cuisine.

Beyond the bustling streets, Phuket revealed its natural wonders. Pristine beaches beckoned sunseekers to lounge on soft sands, while crystal-clear waters invited snorkelers and divers to explore vibrant coral reefs teeming with life. Hidden coves and secret beaches whispered their secrets to those willing to venture off the beaten path, rewarding them with secluded beauty and serenity.

As the day turned into night, Phuket transformed into a playground of excitement and entertainment. Bangla Road, the heartbeat of Phuket's nightlife, came alive with neon lights, pulsating music, and the infectious energy of revelers from every corner of the globe. Cabaret shows dazzled with sparkling costumes and mesmerizing performances, leaving the audience in awe.

But amidst the vibrant nightlife, Phuket also offered moments of tranquility and rejuvenation. Thai massage and wellness centers provided a haven for weary travelers, where skilled hands worked their magic, melting away stress and restoring balance to body and soul.

Phuket was not just an island; it was a gateway to endless adventures. Day trips to nearby islands and national parks unveiled breathtaking landscapes, from towering limestone cliffs to emerald-green lagoons. Elephant sanctuaries and wildlife reserves allowed visitors to connect with nature and support conservation efforts, fostering a deep appreciation for the island's precious ecosystem.

As visitors bid farewell to Phuket, they carried with them cherished memories, stories of laughter, and a deep connection to this tropical haven. Phuket had woven its spell, leaving an indelible mark on their hearts and igniting a desire to return once again.

And so, the story of Phuket continues, welcoming new travelers to uncover its secrets, explore its treasures, and create their own chapters in this paradise on Earth.

1.1 About This Pocket Travel Guide

Welcome to the top-notch travel guide in your pocket for Phuket in 2023! This thorough guide has been created to provide you all the knowledge you need to fully enjoy your time on this stunning island paradise.

Your go-to reference, Phuket: Your Ultimate Pocket Travel Guide for 2023, is crammed with expert advice, thorough suggestions, and insightful information to guarantee a wonderful and well-rounded travel experience. This guide attempts to meet all of your requirements and interests, whether you're a first-time visitor to Phuket or an experienced tourist.

You may discover a wealth of knowledge about Phuket's biggest attractions, gorgeous beaches, colorful culture, outdoor activities, nightlife, food alternatives, and useful pointers for getting around the island on these pages. To provide you access to the most current and accurate information, we have selected the finest of what Phuket has to offer.

This guide's several sections explore various facets of Phuket in order to provide readers a thorough insight of its top attractions. You'll learn about the must-see sights, like as historical sites, temples, and scenic marvels that highlight Phuket's distinctive attractiveness. Discover the ideal place to soak up the sun and take in the turquoise seas by exploring the island's varied beaches, which range from well-known lengths to lesser-known hidden treasures.

We take you on a cultural tour of Phuket, exposing you to regional traditions, celebrations, and the mouthwatering world of Thai food so that you may fully understand what it means to be in Phuket. Discover the thriving nightlife scene, where you can have exotic drinks, dance the night away, and take in mesmerizing shows that combine tradition and contemporary.

We provide a thorough reference to the outdoor activities accessible in Phuket for those looking for adventure. You'll discover a variety of alternatives to satisfy your needs, whether you're an adrenaline addict, a fan of nature, or a water sports fanatic. Phuket has several chances for thrilling adventures, from diving and snorkeling to trekking and exploring the island's gorgeous jungles.

Any trip guide must have useful information, and our pocket guide makes sure you have all the required information close at hand. To guarantee a comfortable and trouble-free vacation, you'll discover helpful advice on modes of transportation, lodging alternatives, eating suggestions, currency conversion, and safety rules.

In addition to the main parts, we've included a special section that leads you off the beaten track and reveals secret attractions and one-of-a-kind experiences that will let you see a side of Phuket that is sometimes ignored by visitors. Explore the island's hidden gems by going off the beaten route; you'll find isolated beaches, real local experiences, and eco-tourism programs that support sustainability.

This compact travel book has been thoughtfully designed to help you plan and enjoy every second of your trip, whether you have a few days or a few weeks to spend in Phuket. Use it as your dependable guide while you explore Phuket's treasures in 2023, consulting it for ideas, direction, and helpful tips.

Prepare yourself for an unforgettable experience as you explore the magnificent beaches, acquaint yourself with the rich culture, and make lifelong memories. This handy travel guide is your key to Phuket's treasures, which are waiting for you.

1.2 How to use of This Guide

Thank you for selecting Phuket: Your Ultimate Pocket Travel Guide for 2023 as your primary guide to discovering this exotic locale. Here's a summary of how to utilize this guide well to help you get the most out of it and your vacation to Phuket:

Become acquainted with the contents: Look through the table of contents for a quick overview of the subjects this manual covers. This will help you organize your exploration of Phuket and give you an idea of the information that is accessible.

Establish Your Priorities: Decide what characteristics of Phuket most appeal to you. Are you more interested in outdoor activities, cultural excursions, beach hopping, or a combination of all of these? By being aware of your preferences, you may concentrate on the areas of the handbook that are relevant to you.

Check out the introduction: You may get an insight of what to anticipate in Phuket by starting with the introduction. It will prepare you for your travel and aid in stoking your excitement for the experiences that lie ahead.

Explore Each Section: Investigate in detail the parts that correspond to your interests. Each section offers insightful information, advice, and suggestions geared to certain facets of Phuket. Immerse yourself in the supplied information to improve your vacation experience, from top sites and beaches to cultural events and nightlife.

Take Note of the Advice: You'll discover suggestions for particular locations to go, things to do, dining establishments, and more inside each area. Write down the suggestions that hit home for you and fit your travel tastes. You will have access to dependable advice thanks to the recommendations of residents and seasoned tourists.

Make Your Travel Plans: Consider making a rough itinerary as you read the book based on the suggestions and sites that you find interesting. This will enable you to plan your days and use your time in Phuket to the most. Travel time, hours of operation, and any other pertinent information stated in the handbook should all be taken into account.

Cross-Reference Useful Information Essential information on travel, lodging, meals, safety, and other topics is provided in the practical information section. While browsing other parts, come return to this one to make sure you have the knowledge you need to go about Phuket easily.

Find Undiscovered Gems: Don't forget to look through the "Off the Beaten Path" area, where you may discover obscure sights, remote beaches, and unusual adventures. You can see a new side of Phuket and make memories that go beyond the conventional tourist sites by visiting these hidden jewels.

Keep This Guide Close by: Carry this pocket handbook with you when touring Phuket for quick access. Pages that are very relevant to your present location or activity should be highlighted or bookmarked. In this manner, you may easily obtain the data you need while on the road.

Customize Your Experience: Keep in mind that this guide is just designed to be a reference; you are free to make Phuket your own. Use the suggestions as a guide, but don't be afraid to explore and find your own favorite locations and activities.

Throughout your trip, Phuket: Your Pocket Travel Guide for 2023 will be at your side, ensuring that you have the information and insights you need to make the most of your stay on the island. Take pleasure in the planning, investigation, and immersion in Phuket's delights. Happy excursions and safe travels!

Phuket Big Buddha

CHAPTER 2: GETTING TO KNOW PHUKET

2.1 Phuket at a Glance

Here's a snapshot of Phuket at a glance to help you get acquainted with this captivating destination:

1. Location: Phuket is situated on the west coast of the Malay Peninsula in southern Thailand. It is approximately 867 kilometers (539 miles) south of Bangkok, the capital city of Thailand.
2. Geography: The island of Phuket spans an area of about 576 square kilometers (222 square miles). It is connected to the mainland by the Sarasin Bridge and is surrounded by the Andaman Sea. Phuket is characterized by its rugged coastline, stunning beaches, lush hills, and inland forests.
3. Population: Phuket is home to a diverse population that includes Thais, as well as a significant expatriate community. The local residents are known for their warm hospitality, making visitors feel welcome and comfortable during their stay.
4. Climate: Phuket has a tropical monsoon climate, with two main seasons: the dry season and the rainy season. Usually from November to April, the dry season is marked by moderate temperatures and low humidity. The rainy season occurs from May to

October, with occasional heavy showers. Phuket's average annual temperature is around 30°C (86°F).

5. Culture: Phuket's culture is a unique blend of Thai, Chinese, and European influences. The majority of the population practices Buddhism, and you'll find numerous temples and shrines throughout the island. Festivals such as Songkran (Thai New Year) and Loy Krathong (Festival of Lights) are celebrated with enthusiasm and provide an opportunity to witness traditional customs and vibrant parades.

6. Language: The official language of Thailand is Thai, and it is widely spoken in Phuket. However, due to the island's popularity among international tourists, English is also commonly spoken, especially in tourist areas, hotels, and restaurants.

7. Currency: The currency in Thailand is the Thai Baht (THB). ATMs are widely available in Phuket, and major credit cards are accepted in most establishments. It's always a good idea to carry some cash for smaller establishments or street markets.

8. Time Zone: Phuket follows Indochina Time (ICT), which is 7 hours ahead of Coordinated Universal Time (UTC+7). It's advisable to adjust your watch and keep track of local time to make the most of your schedule.

These essential details will give you a head start in understanding Phuket's geographical, cultural, and logistical aspects. As you delve deeper into this pocket travel guide, you'll discover more about the island's attractions, activities, and practical information that will make your journey to Phuket even more rewarding.

2.2 History and Culture

Phuket boasts a rich history that has shaped its unique culture and character. The island's strategic location along major trade routes attracted merchants and settlers from various regions, contributing to its diverse cultural heritage. Here's a glimpse into Phuket's fascinating history:

Early History: Phuket's history dates back thousands of years, with evidence of human habitation found as early as the Neolithic period. The island was an important trading hub, frequented by Indian, Arab, and Chinese merchants who sailed through the Andaman Sea.

Influence of the Malay Peninsula and Ayutthaya Kingdom: Phuket's close proximity to the Malay Peninsula had a significant influence on its culture and language. The island came under the influence of the Ayutthaya Kingdom (1351-1767), a powerful Thai empire that played a crucial role in the region's history.

Tin Mining Boom: During the 19th century, Phuket experienced a tin mining boom, attracting Chinese immigrants who settled on the island. The tin industry flourished, bringing wealth and prosperity to Phuket, and the Chinese influence remains prominent in the island's architecture, cuisine, and traditions.

European Influences: European colonial powers, including the Portuguese, Dutch, and British, had a brief presence in Phuket during the Age of Exploration. However, their impact on the island was minimal compared to neighboring regions.

Tsunami and Rebuilding: Phuket faced a devastating tsunami in December 2004, resulting in significant loss of life and infrastructure damage. The local community, along with international support, rallied together to rebuild and restore Phuket, transforming it into a more resilient and vibrant destination.

2.3 Local Customs and Etiquette

To fully appreciate Phuket's culture, it's important to be mindful of local customs and etiquette, Following are some essential ideas to bear in mind:

- Respect for the Monarchy: Thailand holds great reverence for its monarchy. It is important to show respect towards the King, Queen, and royal family. Avoid any disrespectful actions or comments regarding the monarchy.
- Buddhist Traditions: Buddhism is deeply ingrained in Thai culture, and Phuket is home to numerous temples. When visiting temples, dress modestly, remove your shoes before entering, and be mindful of your behavior. It's customary to remain quiet and avoid inappropriate gestures or displays of affection.

- Wai Greeting: The wai is a traditional Thai greeting, where the palms are pressed together in a prayer-like gesture. Thais use the wai to show respect or to greet others. Return the gesture when someone wais you, especially elders or individuals in positions of authority.
- Politeness and Courtesy: Thai people value politeness and courtesy. Use "khap" (for men) or "ka" (for women) as a polite suffix when addressing locals. Be patient, smile, and remain calm even in challenging situations. Keep your voice down and refrain from acting aggressively.
- Social Customs: Phuket has a relaxed atmosphere, but it's essential to be mindful of social norms. A minimum of public affection should be shown. In addition, it's considerate to take off your shoes while entering someone's house or a few other places.

2.4 Weather and Best Time to Visit

Phuket's weather plays a significant role in determining the best time to visit. Here's an overview of the island's climate and the ideal time to plan your trip:

Dry Season (November to April): Sunny days and lesser humidity are characteristics of Phuket's dry season. This is considered the peak tourist season, with December and January being the busiest months. The weather is ideal for beach activities, water sports, and exploring outdoor attractions.

Rainy Season (May to October): The rainy season brings higher humidity and occasional showers to Phuket. However, it's important to note that rain showers are typically short-lived and often followed by sunshine. The upside of visiting during this period is fewer crowds, lower hotel rates, and lush green landscapes.

Best Time to Visit: The best time to visit Phuket depends on your preferences. If you enjoy vibrant nightlife, water activities, and a buzzing atmosphere, the dry season is ideal. For those seeking a quieter experience, the shoulder seasons of May to June and September to October offer a good balance of favorable weather and fewer tourists.

Ultimately, Phuket is a year-round destination, and the best time to visit may vary depending on your personal preferences and interests. Consider the weather, crowd levels, and activities you wish to engage in to determine the perfect time for your Phuket adventure.

Maya bay phi phi island

CHAPTER 3: TOP ATTRACTIONS IN PHUKET

3.1 Old Phuket Town

Located in the heart of Phuket, Old Phuket Town is a vibrant and culturally rich area that offers a fascinating glimpse into the island's past. Here are some highlights of this historical district:

- Colonial Architecture: Stroll along the charming streets of Old Phuket Town and admire the well-preserved Sino-Portuguese architecture. The colorful buildings with their intricate detailing reflect the influence of European colonial powers and create a unique atmosphere.
- Thalang Road and Soi Romanee: Thalang Road is the main thoroughfare of Old Phuket Town and is lined with an array of shops, cafes, and galleries. Soi Romanee, a narrow lane off Thalang Road, showcases beautifully restored shop-houses and is a must-visit for its nostalgic charm.
- Temples and Shrines: Old Phuket Town is home to several Buddhist temples and Chinese shrines. Wat Mongkol Nimit, with its striking red exterior, is a prominent temple in the area. Don't miss the elaborate Jui Tui Shrine, where locals come to offer prayers and seek blessings.

- Local Cuisine: Discover a wealth of culinary delights in Old Phuket Town. Explore the vibrant fresh market, known as Talad Sod Satarana, and sample local street food. From savory noodles and seafood dishes to delectable desserts, the food scene in this area is sure to tantalize your taste buds.
- Art and Culture: The art scene thrives in Old Phuket Town, with numerous galleries showcasing contemporary and traditional artwork. Visit the Phuket Thai Hua Museum, housed in a beautifully restored Chinese school building, to learn about the island's cultural heritage through exhibits and interactive displays.

3.2 Big Buddha

Perched atop Nakkerd Hill, the Big Buddha is an iconic landmark that dominates the Phuket skyline. This impressive statue is a symbol of spirituality and offers breathtaking panoramic views of the island. Here's what you can expect when visiting the Big Buddha:

- Majestic Statue: The Big Buddha stands at an impressive height of 45 meters (147 feet) and is made of white Burmese marble. Its sheer size and serene presence create a sense of awe and reverence.
- Spiritual Significance: The statue holds great religious significance for the local community. It serves as a place of worship and a pilgrimage site for Buddhists. Visitors are welcome to pay their respects and offer prayers at the base of the statue.
- Panoramic Views: Climb the steps to the Big Buddha and be rewarded with breathtaking panoramic views of Phuket's coastline, lush hills, and surrounding islands. The viewpoint provides an excellent photo opportunity and a chance to appreciate the natural beauty of the island.
- Peaceful Atmosphere: The Big Buddha is known for its tranquil ambiance, offering a peaceful respite from the hustle and bustle of daily life. Take a moment to soak in the serenity and enjoy the gentle breeze that often graces the hilltop.
- Adjacent Facilities: Near the Big Buddha, you'll find additional attractions and facilities. Explore the

nearby Wat Chalong, a revered Buddhist temple, and learn about its history and architecture. There are also small shops where you can purchase souvenirs and religious items.

Remember to dress modestly and respectfully when visiting the Big Buddha, as it is a religious site. Cover your shoulders and knees, and remove your shoes before entering any temple areas. Whether you seek spiritual enlightenment or simply want to enjoy the panoramic views, a visit to the Big Buddha is an experience not to be missed in Phuket.

3.3 Wat Chalong

Located in the southern part of Phuket, Wat Chalong is one of the island's most revered Buddhist temples. Known for its intricate architecture and spiritual significance, a visit to Wat Chalong offers a glimpse into the religious heritage of Phuket. Here are the highlights of this sacred site:

- Historical Significance: Wat Chalong holds great historical importance as it played a crucial role during the Chinese Coolie Rebellion in the 19th century. The temple served as a sanctuary for locals seeking refuge and played a pivotal role in resolving the conflict.
- Intricate Architecture: The temple complex features several beautifully adorned buildings and pagodas. Marvel at the ornate details, colorful murals, and intricate woodwork that showcase the artistic craftsmanship of Thai temple architecture.
- Grand Pagoda: The highlight of Wat Chalong is the Grand Pagoda, also known as Phra Mahathat Chedi. This towering structure stands at over 60 meters (197 feet) tall and houses a sacred relic of Lord Buddha. Visitors can climb the stairs to the top for panoramic views of the temple grounds.
- Spiritual Experience: Immerse yourself in the serene atmosphere of Wat Chalong and observe the rituals and practices of devout worshippers. Pay your respects at the various shrines and make merit by lighting incense sticks or leaving offerings.

- Monks' Quarters: Wat Chalong is also home to the monks' quarters, where resident monks reside and carry out their daily activities. Gain insight into the monastic lifestyle and, if appropriate, engage in respectful conversations to learn more about their spiritual practices.

3.4 Phang Nga Bay

Just northeast of Phuket, Phang Nga Bay is a breathtaking natural wonder that enchants visitors with its limestone karsts, emerald-green waters, and picturesque landscapes. Here's what makes Phang Nga Bay a must-visit destination:

- Limestone Karsts and Islands: Phang Nga Bay is renowned for its unique limestone karsts that jut out of the water, creating a stunning and surreal backdrop. Explore the bay's numerous islands, including James Bond Island (featured in the movie "The Man with the Golden Gun"), Koh Panyee, and Koh Hong.
- Sea Cave Exploration: Embark on an adventure through the bay's intricate network of sea caves and hidden lagoons. Explore places like Bat Cave and Diamond Cave, either by sea kayak or with a guided tour, and witness the captivating rock formations and thriving marine ecosystems.
- Panoramic Views: Cruise through Phang Nga Bay and be mesmerized by the panoramic views that unfold before you. The combination of towering limestone cliffs, crystal-clear waters, and verdant mangrove forests creates a visual spectacle that is truly unforgettable.
- Island Hopping and Beaches: Phang Nga Bay offers opportunities for island hopping, allowing you to discover secluded beaches and snorkel in pristine waters. Relax on the soft sands of Naka Island, Lawa Island, or the quieter parts of James Bond Island, and soak up the natural beauty surrounding you.

- Authentic Local Life: Visit Koh Panyee, a unique village built on stilts over the water. Experience the local way of life, explore the floating market, sample fresh seafood dishes, and interact with the friendly villagers who call this place home.

3.5 Phi Phi Islands

The Phi Phi Islands, located a short boat ride away from Phuket, are renowned for their stunning beauty and turquoise waters. These islands, consisting of Phi Phi Don and Phi Phi Leh, offer an idyllic tropical escape. Here's what you can expect:

- Maya Bay and Phi Phi Leh: Phi Phi Leh is home to the famous Maya Bay, a picturesque bay surrounded by towering cliffs and crystal-clear waters. Although Maya Bay is temporarily closed for rehabilitation, you can still admire its beauty from a distance or explore other equally breathtaking beaches on the island.
- Snorkeling and Diving: The Phi Phi Islands are a haven for snorkelers and divers. Discover vibrant coral reefs teeming with marine life, including tropical fish, colorful coral formations, and even turtles. Explore sites like Shark Point, Bida Nok, and Bida Nai for unforgettable underwater adventures.
- Viewpoints and Hiking: Hike up to the viewpoints on Phi Phi Don, such as the Phi Phi Viewpoint and Viewpoint 2, for panoramic vistas of the islands and the surrounding Andaman Sea. These vantage points offer breathtaking views, especially during sunrise and sunset.
- Lively Beaches and Nightlife: Phi Phi Don is known for its lively beaches, such as Tonsai Bay and Loh Dalum Bay, which offer a mix of beachfront bars, restaurants, and entertainment venues. Enjoy the vibrant nightlife, indulge in beach parties, or simply relax with a drink as you soak up the island vibes.
- Island Excursions: Embark on boat excursions around the Phi Phi Islands, allowing you to explore hidden coves, snorkel in secluded bays, and discover lesser-known beaches. Take a long-tail boat or join a tour

to explore the stunning natural landscapes and picturesque spots around the islands.

Note: When visiting the Phi Phi Islands, be respectful of the environment and practice responsible tourism. Help preserve the natural beauty of the islands by following designated trails, properly disposing of waste, and refraining from touching or damaging coral reefs.

3.6 Promthep Cape

Promthep Cape, located on the southern tip of Phuket, is renowned for its panoramic views of the Andaman Sea and spectacular sunsets. Here's what makes Promthep Cape a must-visit destination:

- Scenic Views: Enjoy breathtaking views from the viewpoint at Promthep Cape. The rugged cliffs, crashing waves, and endless expanse of the sea create a dramatic backdrop that is perfect for photography and appreciating the natural beauty of Phuket.
- Sunset Delight: Promthep Cape is famous for its stunning sunsets. As the sun dips below the horizon, the sky transforms into a kaleidoscope of colors, painting the landscape with hues of orange, pink, and purple. Witnessing a sunset at Promthep Cape is a truly magical experience.
- Lighthouse and Cultural Significance: The cape is home to a picturesque red-and-white lighthouse that adds charm to the landscape. The lighthouse serves as a symbol of protection for seafarers and has historical and cultural significance for the local community.
- Walking Trails: Explore the walking trails that lead you along the cliffs, allowing you to soak up the coastal scenery and enjoy peaceful moments in nature. As you meander through the trails, you may encounter local flora and fauna, making it a pleasant excursion for nature enthusiasts.

3.7 Kata Noi Beach

Nestled on the southwestern coast of Phuket, Kata Noi Beach is a pristine and tranquil stretch of sand known for its crystal-clear waters and scenic beauty. Here's why Kata Noi Beach should be on your itinerary:

- Secluded Atmosphere: Kata Noi Beach offers a more relaxed and secluded atmosphere compared to its neighboring beaches. The absence of large crowds

allows you to enjoy a peaceful day by the sea, unwind, and rejuvenate amidst the natural beauty.
- Soft Sands and Azure Waters: Sink your toes into the soft, golden sands of Kata Noi Beach and take a refreshing dip in the clear turquoise waters. The calm and gentle waves make it ideal for swimming, and the beach is well-suited for families and sun-seekers alike.
- Water Sports: Engage in an array of water sports activities available at Kata Noi Beach. Try your hand at snorkeling, kayaking, or even surfing during the right season. Adventure seekers will find plenty of options to make the most of the beach's inviting waters.
- Scenic Views: The beach is framed by lush green hills, creating a picturesque backdrop that enhances the beauty of Kata Noi. Take a leisurely stroll along the shore and relish the stunning coastal scenery, or find a shady spot to sit back and admire the view.
- Dining and Refreshments: Kata Noi Beach is dotted with beachfront restaurants and cafes where you can savor delicious Thai cuisine or enjoy a refreshing drink while taking in the panoramic views. Indulge in a beachside meal and immerse yourself in the laid-back ambiance of the area.

3.8 Patong Beach

Patong Beach, located on the west coast of Phuket, is the island's most popular and vibrant beach destination. Here's what you can expect when visiting Patong Beach:

- Buzzing Atmosphere: Patong Beach is known for its lively and energetic ambiance. The beachfront is lined with hotels, resorts, restaurants, bars, and shops, creating a bustling atmosphere day and night.

It's the perfect destination for those seeking a vibrant and dynamic beach experience.

- Water Activities: Patong Beach offers a wide range of water activities to keep you entertained. From jet skiing and parasailing to banana boat rides and snorkeling, there's no shortage of thrilling adventures to enjoy in the sparkling waters of Patong.
- Beachfront Entertainment: Indulge in beachside relaxation or join in the beach games and activities organized along the shoreline. Sunbathe on the soft sands, rent a beach chair and umbrella, or simply take a leisurely stroll along the lively promenade.
- Shopping and Nightlife: Patong is renowned for its vibrant nightlife and shopping scene. Explore the bustling streets of Bangla Road and the nearby Jungceylon Shopping Center, where you'll find an array of shops, market stalls, and entertainment venues offering a mix of traditional goods and international brands.
- Cultural Experiences: Discover the cultural side of Patong by visiting the Wat Suwan Khiri Khet temple or experiencing the vibrant spectacle of a Thai boxing match at Patong Boxing Stadium. These cultural encounters provide a glimpse into the local way of life amidst the lively beach scene.

3.9 Bangla Road

Bangla Road, located in the heart of Patong Beach, is renowned for its lively nightlife and vibrant entertainment scene. Here's what to expect on this bustling street:

- Nightlife Hub: Bangla Road comes alive after dark, transforming into a vibrant hub of bars, nightclubs, and entertainment venues. The street pulsates with music, neon lights, and enthusiastic revelers,

creating an electrifying atmosphere that is unique to Patong.
- Street Performers and Shows: As you stroll along Bangla Road, you'll encounter street performers showcasing their talents, from live music bands to dancers and fire shows. These captivating performances add to the lively ambiance of the street and provide entertainment for passersby.
- Night Markets and Shopping: Explore the night markets that line Bangla Road, offering a variety of souvenirs, clothing, accessories, and street food. It's a great opportunity to browse for unique items and savor local delicacies while immersing yourself in the energetic vibe of the street.
- International Dining: Bangla Road boasts a wide selection of international restaurants and food stalls, catering to different tastes and preferences. Whether you're craving Thai cuisine, seafood, Italian, Indian, or Japanese, you'll find a diverse range of dining options to satisfy your palate.
- People-Watching and Socializing: Bangla Road is an ideal spot for people-watching and socializing. Grab a seat at one of the outdoor bars or restaurants, order a drink, and watch the lively crowd pass by. Engage in friendly conversations with fellow travelers, making new friends along the way.

Note: Bangla Road's nightlife scene can be lively and energetic, with music, lights, and a bustling crowd. If you prefer a quieter atmosphere, it's advisable to seek accommodation away from the immediate vicinity of Bangla Road.

Patong city, phuket

CHAPTER 4: OVERVIEW OF PHUKET BEACHES

Phuket, the tropical paradise in Thailand, is renowned for its breathtaking beaches that stretch along its coastline. With over 30 stunning beaches to choose from, Phuket offers a diverse range of beach experiences to suit every preference. Here's an overview of the beaches in Phuket:

- Scenic Beauty: Phuket's beaches boast postcard-perfect beauty with their powdery white sands, azure waters, and dramatic landscapes. Many beaches are backed by lush green hills, swaying palm trees, and vibrant tropical vegetation, creating a stunning backdrop for relaxation and enjoyment.
- Activities and Water Sports: Phuket's beaches are not just about sunbathing and swimming. They offer a wealth of water sports and activities to keep visitors entertained. From snorkeling and diving in vibrant coral reefs to jet skiing, parasailing, and banana boat rides, there's no shortage of thrilling adventures for beachgoers.
- Dining and Entertainment: Phuket's beachfront areas are buzzing with a wide array of restaurants, beach clubs, and bars, offering diverse culinary experiences and entertainment options. Whether you crave fresh seafood, authentic Thai cuisine, or international delicacies, you'll find a range of dining establishments to satisfy your taste buds.

- Nightlife and Vibrant Atmosphere: Some of Phuket's beaches come alive after sunset, transforming into vibrant hubs of nightlife and entertainment. Beach areas like Patong Beach and Kata Beach offer a lively ambiance with beach clubs, bars, and nightclubs where you can dance the night away, enjoy live music, or indulge in beachside cocktails.
- Beachfront Relaxation and Serenity: Phuket also caters to those seeking peace and tranquility. Away from the bustling beach areas, you'll find secluded stretches of sand where you can unwind in a serene atmosphere. These beaches provide a peaceful escape, allowing you to immerse yourself in nature, soak up the sun, and enjoy the soothing sound of the waves.
- Variety of Beach Settings: Phuket's beaches come in various sizes and settings, ranging from long and wide expanses of sand to small and secluded coves. Some beaches are easily accessible and well-developed with amenities, while others require a bit of exploration, offering a sense of adventure and discovery.
- Family-Friendly Beaches: Phuket is a popular destination for families, and many of its beaches are ideal for children. The gentle slopes, calm waters, and family-friendly facilities make these beaches safe and enjoyable for kids of all ages. Some beaches even have dedicated play areas and water sports suitable for children.

- Cultural Encounters: Along with their natural beauty, Phuket's beaches provide opportunities for cultural experiences. You may come across local vendors selling traditional handicrafts, beachside massages, or even witness traditional ceremonies or performances near certain beaches.

Whether you're seeking adventure, relaxation, water sports, vibrant nightlife, or simply a tranquil escape, Phuket's beaches offer an incredible range of experiences that cater to every traveler's desires.

4.1 Patong Beach

Patong Beach Patong Beach, located on the west coast of Phuket, is the island's most famous and bustling beach. It is a vibrant and energetic destination that attracts visitors from all over the world. Patong Beach offers a wide stretch of soft, golden sand and clear turquoise waters. The beachfront is lined with numerous hotels, resorts, restaurants, bars, and shops, catering to the needs and preferences of travelers. Patong Beach is known for its lively atmosphere, particularly in the evening, when the area comes alive with vibrant nightlife, street performers, and entertainment shows. Water sports activities such as jet skiing, parasailing, and banana boat rides are also popular at Patong Beach, providing thrill-seekers with an adrenaline-pumping experience. Despite its lively nature, Patong Beach still offers opportunities for relaxation, with designated areas for sunbathing and beachside massages. It is a vibrant and diverse beach destination that appeals to a wide range of travelers.

4.2 Kata Beach

Kata Beach: Kata Beach, located on the southwest coast of Phuket, is a picturesque and family-friendly beach. It offers a more relaxed and laid-back atmosphere compared to Patong Beach, making it an ideal choice for families, couples, and those seeking a quieter beach experience. Kata Beach boasts soft sands, clear waters, and gentle waves, creating a perfect setting for swimming, sunbathing, and water activities. The beach is backed by lush green hills, providing a scenic backdrop that adds to its charm. Kata Beach is also known for its excellent surfing conditions, especially during the monsoon season. Surf schools and equipment rentals are available for those interested in riding the waves. The beach area offers a variety of restaurants, cafes, and shops, where visitors can enjoy delicious Thai cuisine, international dishes, and browse for souvenirs. With its natural beauty and a more relaxed ambiance, Kata Beach offers a peaceful retreat while still providing easy access to amenities and activities.

4.3 Karon Beach

Karon Beach: Karon Beach, located just south of Patong Beach, is the second-largest beach in Phuket. It offers a more tranquil and laid-back atmosphere compared to its neighboring beaches. Karon Beach boasts a long stretch of powdery white sand and crystal-clear waters, creating an inviting environment for beach lovers. The beach is suitable for various activities, including swimming, sunbathing, beach volleyball, and long walks along the shore. Karon Beach is also popular for its stunning sunsets, and many visitors gather along the beach to witness the vibrant colors of the sky as the sun dips below the horizon. The beachfront area features a range of resorts, restaurants, and shops, offering convenience for visitors. While Karon Beach is relatively quieter than Patong Beach, it still provides a selection of dining options, from local eateries serving traditional Thai dishes to international restaurants offering diverse cuisines. Karon Beach is a preferred choice for those seeking a balance between relaxation and accessibility to amenities.

4.4 Kamala Beach

Kamala Beach: Kamala Beach is a tranquil and family-friendly beach located on the west coast of Phuket. It offers a more laid-back and peaceful atmosphere compared to the busier beaches on the island. Kamala Beach features a long stretch of golden sand and clear blue waters, ideal for swimming and sunbathing. The beach is surrounded by lush green hills, creating a picturesque backdrop. Kamala Beach is known for its relaxed vibe and is a popular choice for families seeking a quieter beach experience. There are various beachfront restaurants, cafes, and shops where visitors can enjoy delicious seafood, Thai cuisine, and browse for local handicrafts. Kamala Beach is a charming destination that combines natural beauty with a serene ambiance.

4.5 Surin Beach

Surin Beach: Surin Beach is an upscale and scenic beach located on the west coast of Phuket. It is known for its stunning turquoise waters and powdery white sands, making it a favorite among beach enthusiasts. Surin Beach offers a more exclusive and luxurious experience, with upscale resorts, beach clubs, and restaurants dotting the shoreline. The beach is popular among sunbathers and swimmers, and its gentle waves make it suitable for water activities such as snorkeling and stand-up paddleboarding. Surin Beach provides a serene and sophisticated ambiance, attracting both local and international visitors who appreciate its beauty and upscale offerings.

4.6 Nai Harn Beach

Nai Harn Beach: Nai Harn Beach is a pristine and picturesque beach located on the southern tip of Phuket. It is widely regarded as one of the most beautiful beaches on the island. Nai Harn Beach boasts crystal-clear waters, powdery white sand, and a backdrop of lush green hills. The beach offers a peaceful and unspoiled atmosphere, making it a favorite among nature lovers and those seeking tranquility. The calm waters of Nai Harn Beach are ideal for swimming and snorkeling, while the surrounding park area provides opportunities for hiking and exploring. Nai Harn Beach is a hidden gem that offers natural beauty and a sense of seclusion.

4.7 Freedom Beach

Freedom Beach: Freedom Beach is a hidden gem tucked away on the southwest coast of Phuket. It is accessible only by boat or a steep hiking trail, which adds to its exclusivity and charm. Freedom Beach is known for its pristine beauty, with turquoise waters, soft white sand, and lush greenery surrounding the area. The beach provides a secluded and serene environment, away from the crowds and noise of more popular beaches. In the quiet, beautiful seas, guests may swim, sunbathe, and go snorkeling. There are no beachfront amenities or facilities at Freedom Beach, so it's essential to bring your own supplies for a day trip. The beach's untouched beauty and tranquil atmosphere make it a favorite among nature enthusiasts and those seeking a more secluded beach experience.

4.8 Mai Khao Beach

Mai Khao Beach: Mai Khao Beach is Phuket's longest beach, stretching over 11 kilometers along the northwest coast of the island. It is a pristine and less developed beach known for its natural beauty and tranquility. Mai Khao Beach is part of the Sirinat National Park, ensuring its preservation and protection. The beach offers a serene and peaceful environment, with soft sands and clear waters. It is an excellent spot for long walks, sunbathing, and enjoying the serenity of nature. Mai Khao Beach is also famous as a nesting site for sea turtles, and visitors may have the opportunity to witness these magnificent creatures during nesting seasons. The area surrounding the beach is relatively undeveloped, with only a few resorts and dining options available. Mai Khao Beach is an ideal choice for those seeking a pristine and unspoiled beach experience away from the crowds.

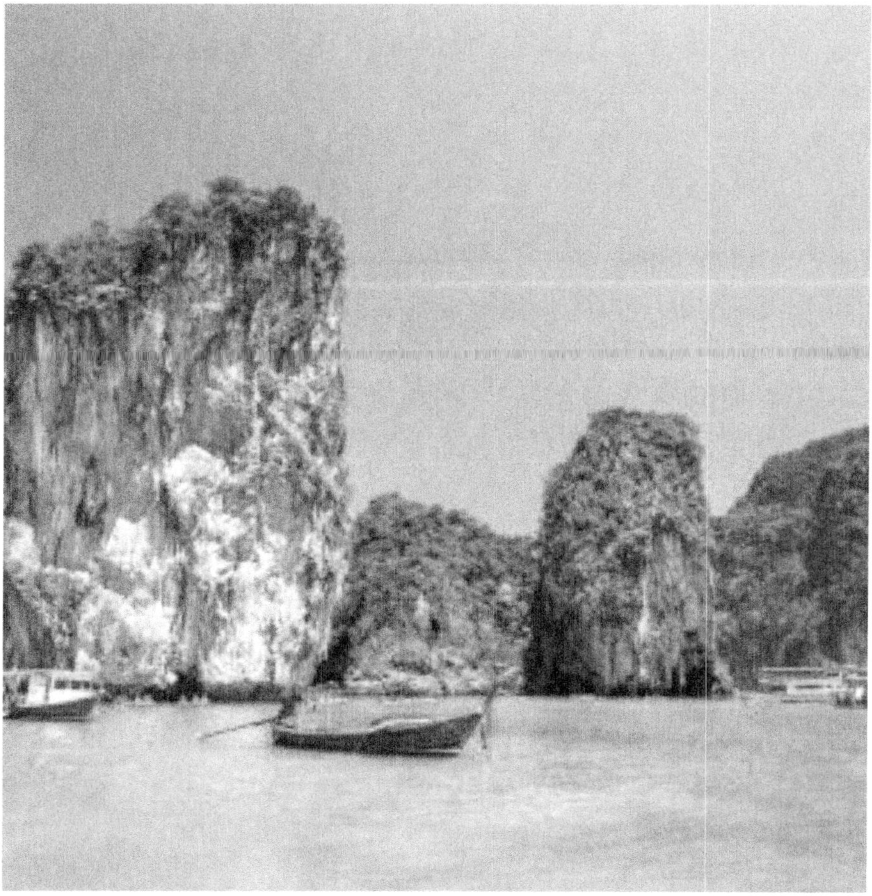

CHAPTER 5: EXPLORING PHUKET'S CULTURE

5.1 Temples and Shrines

5.1 Temples and Shrines: Phuket is not only known for its stunning beaches but also for its rich cultural heritage. Exploring the temples and shrines on the island offers a glimpse into the spiritual and religious traditions of the local Thai people. Here are some notable temples and shrines worth visiting:

- Wat Chalong: One of the most important and revered temples in Phuket, Wat Chalong is a magnificent complex that showcases exquisite architecture and intricate artwork. It is a center of Buddhist worship and houses several statues and relics, including the famous Grand Pagoda that contains a bone fragment of Lord Buddha.
- Big Buddha: Located atop Nakkerd Hill, the Big Buddha is a towering statue that stands at 45 meters tall. It is an iconic landmark of Phuket and offers panoramic views of the island. Visitors can make their way up the hill to admire the statue up close and enjoy the serene atmosphere of the surrounding area.
- Wat Phra Thong: Known as the Temple of the Golden Buddha, Wat Phra Thong is famous for its half-buried golden Buddha statue. Legend has it that

anyone who tries to remove the statue is met with misfortune, thus earning the temple its unique name. It is an interesting and mystical site to explore.
- Wat Srisoonthorn: This temple is notable for its serene and peaceful ambiance. It houses a large reclining Buddha statue and beautiful murals depicting Buddhist stories. The temple grounds are well-maintained and provide a tranquil setting for meditation and reflection.
- Shrine of the Serene Light: Situated near Phuket Town, this Chinese shrine is dedicated to the Goddess Kuan Yin. It is adorned with intricate decorations and colorful sculptures, and it serves as a place of worship for the local Chinese community. The shrine is a fascinating blend of Chinese and Thai cultural elements.

5.2 Traditional Festivals and Events

5.2 Traditional Festivals and Events: Phuket is home to several vibrant and colorful festivals and events that celebrate the island's cultural heritage. Participating in these festivities provides a unique opportunity to immerse oneself in the local culture. Here are a few noteworthy festivals and events in Phuket:

- Songkran: Celebrated in April, Songkran is the Thai New Year festival and is marked by lively water fights and religious ceremonies. Locals and visitors take to

the streets armed with water guns and buckets, joyfully splashing water on each other to symbolize the cleansing of the past year.
- Vegetarian Festival: Held in September or October, the Vegetarian Festival is a significant event for Phuket's Chinese community. Devotees practice a strict vegetarian diet and engage in ritualistic acts of self-mortification, including body piercing and walking on hot coals, to cleanse the body and bring good fortune.
- Loy Krathong: Taking place on the full moon night of the 12th lunar month (usually in November), Loy Krathong is a festival celebrated nationwide in Thailand. In Phuket, locals and visitors gather near water bodies to release intricately crafted banana leaf floats, known as "krathongs," decorated with candles, incense, and flowers, as a gesture of respect to the water spirits and to make wishes for the coming year.
- Phuket Old Town Festival: This annual festival, held in February, celebrates the rich history and cultural heritage of Phuket Town. The streets come alive with vibrant parades, traditional performances, street food stalls, and various cultural activities. It's a great opportunity to explore the town's Sino-Portuguese architecture, sample local delicacies, and enjoy the lively atmosphere.

These temples and festivals provide an immersive experience into Phuket's rich cultural tapestry, allowing visitors to appreciate the spiritual beliefs, customs, and traditions that shape the island's identity.

5.3 Local Cuisine and Street Food

5.3 Local Cuisine and Street Food: Exploring Phuket's local cuisine and street food is a must for food lovers. The island offers a delectable array of flavors and dishes that showcase the diversity of Thai cuisine. Here are some highlights:

- Thai Street Food: Wander through the bustling streets of Phuket and indulge in the vibrant street food scene. From aromatic and spicy curries to flavorful stir-fried noodles, you'll find an abundance of food stalls and carts offering an extensive range of Thai delicacies. Don't miss favorites like Pad Thai, Tom Yum Goong, Satay, and Mango Sticky Rice.
- Seafood Delights: Phuket's coastal location means an abundance of fresh seafood. Head to the local seafood markets or beachfront restaurants to savor dishes like grilled prawns, steamed fish, crab curry, and shellfish. Raw oysters and grilled squid are also popular choices.
- Local Specialties: Phuket has its own unique dishes worth trying. Look out for Mee Hokkien (Hokkien noodles), a stir-fried noodle dish with pork, seafood, and vegetables, or Moo Hong (braised pork belly), a

- flavorful and tender pork dish cooked with soy sauce and spices.
- Night Markets: Visit the vibrant night markets in Phuket to experience a feast for the senses. These markets offer a wide range of street food vendors, showcasing local dishes and snacks. Try grilled meats, savory pancakes, fresh fruits, and Thai desserts. The markets also offer clothing, accessories, and souvenirs to explore.

5.4 Night Markets and Shopping

5.4 Night Markets and Shopping: Phuket is a shopper's paradise, offering a variety of shopping experiences to suit every taste and budget. Here are some highlights:

- Night Markets: Phuket's night markets are not just about food; they are also great places to shop for bargains. Popular night markets include Phuket Weekend Market (also known as Naka Market), Chillva Market, and Malin Plaza. These markets offer a range of clothing, accessories, handicrafts, and souvenirs. Bargaining is common, so brush up on your haggling skills.
- Shopping Malls: Phuket is home to several modern shopping malls that provide a comfortable and air-conditioned shopping experience. Central Festival Phuket, Jungceylon Shopping Mall, and Central Patong are among the most popular malls. They

- feature international brands, local boutiques, entertainment options, and food courts.
- Local Markets: Explore local markets like Phuket Walking Street, Banzaan Fresh Market, and Karon Market to immerse yourself in the local shopping scene. These markets offer a variety of goods, including fresh produce, clothing, accessories, and souvenirs. It's a great way to interact with locals and experience the local lifestyle.
- Boutique Stores: Phuket is also known for its boutique stores and designer shops, particularly in areas like Phuket Old Town and Cherngtalay. These stores offer unique fashion items, handmade crafts, jewelry, and home decor.

5.5 Thai Massage and Wellness

5.5 Thai Massage and Wellness: Phuket is a haven for relaxation and wellness, offering a wide range of spas and wellness centers. Here's what you can expect:

- Traditional Thai Massage: Treat yourself to a traditional Thai massage, a therapeutic practice that combines acupressure, stretching, and deep tissue massage techniques. Numerous spas and massage parlors throughout Phuket offer this rejuvenating experience.
- Spa Retreats: Pamper yourself at one of Phuket's luxurious spa retreats. From holistic wellness centers to beachfront spa resorts, you'll find a range of

treatments, including aromatherapy, body scrubs, facials, and traditional Thai herbal compress massages.
- Yoga and Meditation: Phuket has a growing yoga and meditation scene. Many resorts and wellness centers offer yoga classes and workshops suitable for all levels. Join a session to relax your mind, improve flexibility, and restore balance to your body.
- Detox and Wellness Programs: Phuket is known for its detox and wellness programs that offer a holistic approach to health. These programs typically include activities such as yoga, meditation, detoxifying treatments, and healthy cuisine, allowing you to rejuvenate your body and mind.

Phuket's local cuisine, street food, shopping opportunities, and wellness offerings contribute to a holistic experience that allows visitors to indulge in the island's vibrant culture and take care of their well-being.

CHAPTER 6: OUTDOOR ACTIVITIES IN PHUKET

6.1 Island Hopping and Snorkeling

6.1 Island Hopping and Snorkeling: Phuket is surrounded by breathtakingly beautiful islands and crystal-clear waters, offering a paradise for island hopping and snorkeling enthusiasts. Here are some leisure activities you may engage in outside:

- Island Hopping: Embark on a boat tour and explore the nearby islands around Phuket. Popular destinations include the Phi Phi Islands, Similan Islands, Racha Islands, and Coral Island. Hop from one island to another, discovering pristine beaches, hidden coves, and vibrant marine life.
- Snorkeling: Put on your snorkeling gear and dive into the warm waters surrounding Phuket. Explore colorful coral reefs, encounter tropical fish, and witness the diverse marine ecosystem up close. Snorkeling spots such as Shark Point, Banana Beach, and Paradise Beach offer excellent opportunities to observe underwater wonders.
- Kayaking and Paddleboarding: Rent a kayak or paddleboard and explore the calm bays and mangrove forests of Phuket. Glide through the emerald waters, paddle along the coastline, and

soak in the natural beauty that surrounds you. It's a peaceful and enjoyable way to connect with nature.
- Sunset Cruises: Experience the magic of a sunset cruise in Phuket. Sail along the coastline, enjoying breathtaking views as the sun sets over the Andaman Sea. Some cruises also offer dinner and entertainment options, making it a memorable and romantic experience.

6.2 Scuba Diving and Underwater Exploration

6.2 Scuba Diving and Underwater Exploration: Phuket is renowned as a world-class scuba diving destination, attracting divers from around the globe. Here are some highlights for scuba diving and underwater exploration:

- Dive Sites: Phuket is surrounded by exceptional dive sites, each with its unique underwater landscapes and marine life. Popular dive sites include the Similan Islands, Surin Islands, Shark Point, and the King Cruiser Wreck. Explore vibrant coral reefs, encounter colorful tropical fish, and, if you're lucky, spot majestic manta rays and whale sharks.
- Diving Courses: Whether you're a beginner or an experienced diver, Phuket offers a range of diving courses suited to different skill levels. Professional dive centers and instructors provide training and certification programs, allowing you to explore the underwater world safely.

- Liveaboard Diving: For a more immersive diving experience, consider joining a liveaboard trip. These multi-day excursions take you to remote dive sites and offer the opportunity to dive multiple times a day. Liveaboard trips often visit the renowned Similan Islands and offer a chance to encounter larger marine species.
- Underwater Photography: Capture the beauty of Phuket's underwater world by indulging in underwater photography. Many dive centers offer photography courses and rental equipment, allowing you to capture stunning images of marine life, vibrant corals, and the captivating underwater scenery.

Phuket's outdoor activities provide endless opportunities for adventure, exploration, and connecting with nature. Whether you choose to go island hopping, snorkeling, scuba diving, or simply enjoy a relaxing sunset cruise, the natural beauty of Phuket's surroundings will leave you with unforgettable memories.

6.3 Surfing and Watersports

- 6.3 Surfing and Watersports: Phuket's coastline offers fantastic opportunities for surfing and various watersports, catering to both beginners and experienced enthusiasts. Here are some activities to enjoy:

Phuket A Pocket Travel Guide 2023

- Surfing: Head to popular surf spots like Kata Beach, Kalim Beach, and Nai Harn Beach, where you can catch waves and ride the surf. Lessons and equipment rentals are available for those new to surfing, while experienced surfers can enjoy the challenge of the waves.
- Stand-Up Paddleboarding (SUP): Explore Phuket's calm bays and mangrove forests on a stand-up paddleboard. SUP is a great way to enjoy the tranquility of the water while improving your balance and core strength.
- Jet Skiing and Parasailing: If you're seeking an adrenaline rush, try jet skiing or parasailing along Phuket's beaches. Speed across the water on a jet ski or soar high above the sea while parasailing, enjoying the breathtaking views.
- Wakeboarding and Water Skiing: Test your skills on a wakeboard or water skis as you glide through the water and feel the thrill of being towed by a speedboat. Several locations around Phuket offer these exhilarating activities.

6.4 Hiking and Nature Trails

- 6.4 Hiking and Nature Trails: Phuket is not just about its beaches; it also boasts lush forests, hills, and nature trails, providing excellent opportunities for hiking and nature enthusiasts. Here's what you can explore:

- Khao Phra Thaeo National Park: Located in the northeast part of the island, this park is home to lush rainforests, waterfalls, and diverse wildlife. Hike through the trails, visit the Bang Pae Waterfall, and spot various species of flora and fauna.
- Promthep Cape: Known for its stunning panoramic views, Promthep Cape offers an easy hiking trail that takes you to the cape's viewpoint. Witness breathtaking sunsets and enjoy the beauty of the surrounding landscape.
- Sirinat National Park: Located near Phuket International Airport, this park offers nature trails and a peaceful atmosphere. Explore the coastal mangrove forests, relax on secluded beaches, and observe the diverse bird species that inhabit the area.
- Bang Pae Waterfall and Ton Sai Waterfall: These picturesque waterfalls provide refreshing spots for a hike and a dip in the natural pools. Enjoy the serenity of the forested surroundings as you trek to these cascades.

6.5 Elephant Sanctuaries and Wildlife Reserves

6.5 Elephant Sanctuaries and Wildlife Reserves: For those interested in wildlife conservation and experiencing close encounters with animals, Phuket offers opportunities to visit ethical elephant sanctuaries and wildlife reserves. Here's what you can expect:

- Elephant Sanctuaries: Choose an ethical elephant sanctuary that focuses on the well-being and conservation of these gentle giants. Interact with elephants in a responsible and respectful manner, feed them, bathe them, and learn about their behavior and conservation efforts.
- Gibbon Rehabilitation Project: Visit the Gibbon Rehabilitation Project in Phuket, which aims to rescue and rehabilitate gibbons that have been kept as pets or used in the tourism industry. Observe these fascinating primates and learn about the efforts to reintroduce them to the wild.
- Phuket Zoo and Aquarium: While controversial, Phuket Zoo and Aquarium provide opportunities to observe a variety of animal species up close. However, it is essential to research the ethical practices and treatment of animals before visiting such establishments.

Remember to prioritize responsible tourism and choose activities and sanctuaries that promote the well-being and conservation of animals.

Phuket offers a diverse range of outdoor activities, catering to different interests and adventure levels. Whether you're seeking the thrill of surfing and watersports, the tranquility of hiking and nature trails, or the unique experience of interacting with elephants and observing wildlife, Phuket has something for everyone to enjoy.

Night market in phuket

CHAPTER 7: NIGHTLIFE AND ENTERTAINMENT

7.1 Bangla Road

7.1 Bangla Road: Phuket's Entertainment Hub When the sun sets, Phuket comes alive with its vibrant nightlife, and at the heart of it all is Bangla Road. Located in Patong, Bangla Road is the epicenter of entertainment and excitement. Here's what you can expect:

- Neon Lights and Energy: Bangla Road is a bustling street that comes alive with dazzling neon lights, music, and a vibrant atmosphere. As you walk down the road, you'll be immersed in a sensory experience of sights and sounds.
- Bars and Clubs: Bangla Road is lined with numerous bars and clubs, offering a diverse range of music, drinks, and entertainment. From live music venues and sports bars to pulsating nightclubs, there's something for everyone's taste.
- Night Markets: Alongside the bars and clubs, you'll also find night markets offering a variety of street food, souvenirs, clothing, and accessories. Take a break from the energetic nightlife and explore the stalls to savor local delicacies or shop for unique items.
- Street Performers: Bangla Road is known for its street performers who showcase their talents

throughout the night. From fire dancers and acrobats to live bands and DJs, these performers add an extra element of excitement and entertainment to the bustling street.

7.2 Nightclubs and Bars

7.2 Nightclubs and Bars: Phuket's nightlife extends beyond Bangla Road, with a wide selection of nightclubs and bars scattered throughout the island. Here are some popular options:

- Illuzion Phuket: Located in Patong, Illuzion is one of Phuket's largest and most renowned nightclubs. With its state-of-the-art sound and lighting systems, international DJs, and pulsating dance floors, it offers an unforgettable clubbing experience.
- White Room Nightclub: Situated in Patong, White Room is known for its sleek and stylish ambiance, featuring top-notch DJs and a diverse music selection. Both residents and visitors alike like visiting this location.
- Seduction Nightclub: Another prominent nightlife venue in Patong, Seduction offers multiple rooms playing different genres of music, ensuring there's something for everyone. It's a hotspot for partygoers looking to dance the night away.
- Rooftop Bars: Phuket also boasts several rooftop bars that offer panoramic views of the city and the Andaman Sea. Enjoy a cocktail while taking in the

breathtaking scenery at venues like Baba Nest, Catch Beach Club, or 360° Bar at The Pavilions Phuket.
- Beach Clubs: Phuket's beach clubs combine sun, sand, and music to create a unique party experience. Places like Catch Beach Club, Dream Beach Club, and XANA Beach Club offer beachside lounging, pool parties, live DJs, and a lively atmosphere.

Note: It's important to drink responsibly and be aware of your surroundings while enjoying Phuket's nightlife. Stay hydrated, look after your belongings, and consider using reputable transportation options when moving between venues.

Phuket's nightlife scene offers endless possibilities for entertainment and enjoyment. Whether you're seeking the energetic atmosphere of Bangla Road or the sophistication of rooftop bars and beach clubs, you're sure to find a venue that suits your preferences and ensures a memorable night out.

7.3 Cabaret Shows and Ladyboy Performances

7.3 Cabaret Shows and Ladyboy Performances: Phuket is famous for its dazzling cabaret shows and ladyboy performances that showcase the beauty, talent, and charm of transgender artists. Here's what you can expect:

- Simon Cabaret: Located in Patong, Simon Cabaret is one of the most renowned cabaret shows in Phuket. The show features extravagant costumes, stunning

sets, and mesmerizing performances by talented ladyboy artists. Prepare to be entertained by dance routines, comedy acts, and glamorous performances.
- Aphrodite Cabaret Show: Another popular cabaret show in Phuket, Aphrodite Cabaret Show offers a mix of extravagant performances, lively music, and dazzling costumes. Enjoy a night of glitz and glamour as the performers take the stage with their impressive talents.
- Cultural Performances: In addition to cabaret shows, Phuket also offers cultural performances that showcase traditional Thai dances, music, and martial arts. Experience the rich heritage of Thailand through these captivating performances that often take place in cultural centers or dinner theaters.

7.4 Beach Parties and Fire Shows

7.4 Beach Parties and Fire Shows: Phuket's beach parties and fire shows provide a unique blend of entertainment and tropical vibes. Here are some things to anticipate:

- Patong Beach Parties: Patong Beach is renowned for its lively beach parties that take place throughout the year, particularly during the high season. Dance to the beats of international DJs, enjoy live music performances, and mingle with fellow partygoers on the sandy shores of Patong.

- Fire Shows: Many beach clubs and bars in Phuket feature mesmerizing fire shows that add an extra element of excitement to the nightlife scene. Watch skilled performers twirl fire poi, breathe fire, and create dazzling fire displays that will leave you in awe.
- Full Moon Parties: While the famous Full Moon Party in Koh Phangan is well-known, Phuket also hosts its own version of this lively event. Enjoy a night of music, dancing, and beachside revelry under the light of the full moon.

7.5 Live Music and Cultural Performances

7.5 Live Music and Cultural Performances: Phuket offers a range of venues where you can enjoy live music and cultural performances. Here are some options:

- Live Music Bars: Phuket is home to numerous live music bars where talented local bands and musicians showcase their skills. From rock and reggae to jazz and pop, you can find a variety of genres to suit your taste. Explore areas like Patong, Kata, and Old Phuket Town to discover lively music scenes.
- Cultural Shows: Immerse yourself in Thai culture by attending cultural shows that feature traditional music, dance, and performances. These shows often incorporate elements of Thai folklore, history, and artistry, offering a captivating glimpse into the country's heritage.

- Street Performers: As you wander through the streets of Phuket, you may come across street performers showcasing their talents. From buskers playing musical instruments to artists painting live portraits, these impromptu performances add a touch of artistic charm to the city.

Phuket's nightlife and entertainment options cater to diverse interests, offering a blend of vibrant cabaret shows, beach parties, live music, and cultural performances. Whether you choose to be captivated by the talents of ladyboy performers, dance under the stars at a beach party, or appreciate the melodies of live music, Phuket's nightlife scene promises an unforgettable experience.

CHAPTER 8: PRACTICAL INFORMATION

8.1 Transportation in Phuket

8.1 Transportation in Phuket: Getting around Phuket is relatively easy, thanks to various transportation options available. Here's what you need to know:

- Taxis: Taxis are a convenient way to travel around Phuket. They may be hailed from the street or found at taxi stands. Ensure that the meter is used or negotiate the fare before starting the journey. Taxis in Phuket are usually color-coded, with red and yellow being the most common.
- Tuk-tuks: Tuk-tuks are three-wheeled motorized vehicles that are a popular mode of transportation in Phuket. They are often brightly decorated and offer a unique and fun way to get around. However, fares are usually negotiated, so be prepared to haggle and agree on a price before hopping on.
- Motorbike Taxis: If you're traveling alone or with a companion and want a quicker way to navigate through traffic, motorbike taxis are a popular option. They can be found at designated stands and are recognized by their colored vests. Negotiate the fare in advance and don't forget to wear a helmet for safety.

- Rental Scooters: Renting a scooter is a popular choice for many visitors in Phuket. It allows for more flexibility and the freedom to explore the island at your own pace. However, make sure you have the necessary driving license, wear a helmet, and exercise caution while driving, as traffic conditions can be challenging.
- Songthaews are modified pickup trucks that have covered seats in the rear. They serve as shared taxis or mini-buses, following specific routes around the island. Look for the color-coded signs indicating the destinations they serve. Songthaews are an affordable option for short to medium distances.
- Public Buses: Phuket also has a public bus system that connects various parts of the island. The buses are relatively inexpensive, but the routes and schedules may be less frequent or convenient for tourists. They can be a viable option if you're traveling on a budget or prefer a more local experience.
- Car Rental: Renting a car is an excellent choice if you prefer the convenience of having your own vehicle. Several car rental companies operate in Phuket, and having a car allows you to explore the island more independently. Ensure you have a valid driver's license and be aware of the traffic rules and driving conditions.
- Grab and Other Ride-Hailing Apps: Grab, a popular ride-hailing app in Southeast Asia, operates in

Phuket. It offers convenient and transparent pricing for taxi rides, making it a reliable option for transportation.

Remember to plan your transportation options based on your itinerary and the locations you intend to visit. Consider the distance, time, and convenience when choosing the most suitable mode of transport. It's also worth noting that traffic in popular areas like Patong can be congested, especially during peak tourist seasons.

8.2 Accommodation Options

8.2 Accommodation Options: Phuket offers a wide range of accommodation options to suit various budgets and preferences. Here are some popular choices:

TOP HOTELS IN PHUKET

1. The Beachfront Hotel Phuket

The Beachfront Hotel Phuket is a stunning accommodation nestled in the heart of Warsaw, offering guests a unique and luxurious beachfront experience. With its prime location and exquisite amenities, it promises an unforgettable stay for both leisure and business travelers.

Property Amenities:

- Direct access to a pristine sandy beach with breathtaking views of the ocean.

- For leisure, there is an outdoor swimming pool with lounge seats and umbrellas.
- Spa and wellness center offering a range of rejuvenating treatments and massages.
- Fitness center equipped with state-of-the-art exercise machines for health enthusiasts.
- Multiple on site dining options serving delicious international and local cuisine.
- Conference and meeting facilities for business events and gatherings.
- 24-hour front desk service and concierge assistance for guests' convenience.
- Complimentary Wi-Fi access available throughout the property.

Room Features:

- Luxurious and well-appointed rooms with modern decor and soothing color schemes.
- Private balconies or terraces offering panoramic views of the beach or city skyline.
- Comfortable mattresses with high-quality linen for a good night's sleep.
- Air conditioning and soundproofing for a peaceful and comfortable stay.

- Entertainment options include flat-screen TVs with cable.Mini-bar, coffee/tea making facilities, and in-room dining options for added convenience.
- En-suite bathrooms with rainfall showers, complimentary toiletries, and plush bathrobes.
- Work desk and seating area for business travelers or those needing a dedicated workspace.

Room Types:

- Deluxe Ocean View Room: Enjoy stunning views of the ocean from the comfort of your room.
- Superior City View Room: Admire the vibrant cityscape of Warsaw from your private balcony.
- Junior Suite: Spacious suites with a separate living area for enhanced comfort and relaxation.
- Executive Suite: Indulge in luxury with extra space, a separate bedroom, and upgraded amenities.

Good to Know:

- The Beachfront Hotel Phuket offers a complimentary shuttle service to and from the airport for guests' convenience.
- A range of water sports activities, such as snorkeling and kayaking, can be arranged at the hotel's beachfront.

- The hotel's concierge can assist with arranging city tours, restaurant reservations, and ticket bookings for local attractions.
- The hotel is located near popular shopping and dining destinations, allowing guests to explore the vibrant neighborhood easily.
- Complimentary breakfast is served daily, offering a variety of options to suit different dietary preferences.

The Beachfront Hotel Phuket in Warsaw is a haven of relaxation and luxury, combining beachfront tranquility with the vibrant energy of the city. With its exceptional property amenities, well-appointed rooms, and a range of room types to choose from, it caters to the needs of every traveler. Whether you seek a romantic getaway, a family vacation, or a productive business trip, this hotel promises an exceptional experience.

2. Hotel Clover Patong Phuket

Hotel Clover Patong Phuket is a charming and contemporary hotel located in the heart of Patong Beach, Phuket. With its stylish design, comfortable accommodations, and convenient location, it offers a delightful stay for travelers seeking both relaxation and excitement.

Property Amenities:

- Rooftop swimming pool with panoramic views of Patong Beach and the surrounding area.
- Poolside bar offering refreshing drinks and light snacks.
- On-site restaurant serving a variety of local and international cuisine.
- Modern workout equipment is available at the fitness facility for those who want to keep active.
- 24-hour front desk service and concierge assistance for any inquiries or requests.
- Complimentary Wi-Fi access available throughout the property.
- Airport shuttle service for convenient transportation to and from the hotel.
- For the convenience of the visitors, laundry and dry cleaning services.

Room Features:

- Well-appointed and stylishly designed rooms with modern furnishings.
- Comfortable beds with quality bedding for a restful sleep.
- own patios or balconies with views of the neighborhood.

- Air conditioning and soundproofing for a peaceful and comfortable stay.
- Flat-screen TVs with cable channels for entertainment.
- Mini-bar, coffee/tea making facilities, and in-room dining options for added convenience.
- En suite bathrooms with rainfall showers, complimentary toiletries, and hairdryers.
- Work desk and seating area in select rooms for business travelers or those needing a dedicated workspace.

Room Types:

- Superior Room: Cozy and comfortable room with modern amenities and a choice of a king or twin beds.
- Deluxe Room: Spacious room with additional seating area and a choice of a king or twin beds.
- Family Room: Ideal for families, featuring multiple beds and a separate living area.
- Suite: Luxurious and spacious suite with a separate living area and a private balcony.

Good to Know:

- The hotel is conveniently located within walking distance of Patong Beach, shopping centers, and vibrant nightlife.
- The hotel offers tour desk services to assist guests in arranging excursions, island tours, and activities.
- Complimentary breakfast is served daily, offering a variety of options to start the day.
- The hotel provides 24-hour security to ensure the safety and comfort of guests.
- The friendly and attentive staff are available to assist guests with any needs or recommendations.

Hotel Clover Patong Phuket offers a comfortable and convenient retreat in the heart of Patong Beach. With its range of amenities, stylish rooms, and friendly service, it is an ideal choice for both leisure and business travelers seeking a memorable stay in Phuket.

3. Chanalai Flora Resort, Kata Beach, Phuket

Chanalai Flora Resort is a tropical haven located in the beautiful Kata Beach area of Phuket, Thailand. With its serene ambiance, lush surroundings, and proximity to the beach, it offers a perfect retreat for those seeking relaxation and tranquility.

Property Amenities:

- Outdoor swimming pool surrounded by tropical gardens, sun loungers, and a poolside bar.
- On-site restaurant offering a variety of local and international cuisine.
- Modern workout equipment is available at the fitness facility for those who want to keep active.
- 24-hour front desk service and concierge assistance for any inquiries or requests.
- Spa and wellness center offering a range of rejuvenating treatments and massages.
- Complimentary Wi-Fi access available throughout the property.
- Airport shuttle service for convenient transportation to and from the resort.
- Laundry and dry-cleaning services for guests' convenience.

Room Features:

- Well-appointed and comfortable rooms with modern amenities and a tropical touch.
- Balcony or terrace in select rooms, offering views of the resort's gardens or pool area.
- Air conditioning and ceiling fans for a pleasant and cool environment.

- Flat-screen TVs with cable channels for entertainment.
- Mini-bar, coffee/tea making facilities, and in-room dining options for added convenience.
- En-suite bathrooms with showers, complimentary toiletries, and hairdryers.
- Work desk and seating area in select rooms for business travelers or those needing a dedicated workspace.

Room Types:

- Superior Room: Cozy and comfortable room with a choice of a king or twin beds.
- Deluxe Room: Spacious room with additional seating area and a choice of a king or twin beds.
- Pool Access Room: Direct access to the swimming pool from the private terrace.
- Family Room: Ideal for families, featuring multiple beds and a separate living area.

Good to Know:

- The resort is located a short walk away from the beautiful Kata Beach, known for its clear waters and stunning sunsets.

- Guests can enjoy nearby water sports activities, such as snorkeling, diving, and surfing.
- The resort offers a tour desk to assist guests in arranging excursions, island tours, and activities.
- Complimentary breakfast is served daily, offering a variety of options to start the day.
- The resort provides 24 hour security to ensure the safety and comfort of guests.
- The friendly and attentive staff are available to assist guests with any needs or recommendations.

Chanalai Flora Resort offers a serene and tropical escape in the heart of Kata Beach. With its range of amenities, comfortable rooms, and proximity to the beach, it is an ideal choice for travelers seeking a peaceful and memorable stay in Phuket.

Top hostels to stays in Phuket

1. Lub d Phuket Patong

Lub d Phuket Patong is a vibrant and stylish hostel located in the heart of Patong Beach, Phuket, Thailand. With its modern design, social atmosphere, and convenient location, it offers a fun and affordable stay for budget-conscious travelers.

Property Amenities:

- Rooftop swimming pool with panoramic views of Patong Beach and the surrounding area.
- On-site bar and lounge area, perfect for socializing and meeting fellow travelers.
- Communal kitchen and dining area for guests to prepare and enjoy their own meals.
- Game room with various entertainment options, including board games and pool tables.
- 24-hour front desk service and friendly staff to assist with any inquiries or requests.
- Co-working space with high-speed internet access for digital nomads and remote workers.
- Complimentary Wi-Fi available throughout the property.
- Laundry facilities for guests' convenience.

- Tour desk to help guests arrange excursions, island tours, and activities.

Room Features:

- Comfortable bunk beds with individual reading lights, privacy curtains, and personal lockers.
- Air conditioning and fans in the rooms for a comfortable stay.
- Shared bathrooms with hot showers and complimentary toiletries.
- Power outlets and USB charging ports for each bed.
- In-room safes to store valuables.

Room Types:

- Mixed Dormitory: Shared dormitory room with bunk beds and shared bathrooms.
- Female Dormitory: Shared dormitory room exclusively for female guests with bunk beds and shared bathrooms.

Good to Know:

- Lub d Phuket Patong offers a social and lively atmosphere, perfect for solo travelers or those looking to meet fellow adventurers.

- The hostel is located in close proximity to Patong Beach, shopping centers, and vibrant nightlife.
- Complimentary breakfast is served daily, offering a selection of light bites and beverages.
- The hostel organizes social events and activities, providing opportunities for guests to connect and explore together.
- The friendly staff are available to provide recommendations on local attractions, dining options, and nightlife.

Lub d Phuket Patong is an exciting and affordable choice for travelers seeking a vibrant and social experience in Patong Beach. With its convenient amenities, comfortable dormitory rooms, and welcoming atmosphere, it is the ideal base for exploring Phuket on a budget.

2. The Luna Hostel

The Luna Hostel is a cozy and welcoming accommodation located in a vibrant neighborhood of Phuket, Thailand. With its friendly atmosphere, comfortable facilities, and convenient location, it offers a budget-friendly stay for travelers seeking a relaxed and social experience.

Property Amenities:

- Common lounge area for guests to relax, socialize, and meet fellow travelers.

- Communal kitchen and dining area for guests to prepare and enjoy their own meals.
- Outdoor terrace or garden where guests can unwind and soak up the tropical ambiance.
- 24-hour front desk service with helpful staff available to assist with inquiries and recommendations.
- Free Wi-Fi access available throughout the property.
- Laundry facilities for guests' convenience.
- Tour desk to help guests arrange excursions, activities, and transportation.

Room Features:

- Comfortable bunk beds with individual reading lights and personal lockers for each guest.
- Air conditioning or fans in the rooms for a comfortable stay.
- Shared bathrooms with hot showers and complimentary toiletries.
- Power outlets and USB charging ports near each bed.
- Bed linens and towels provided for guests.

Room Types:

- Mixed Dormitory: Shared dormitory room with bunk beds and shared bathrooms.
- Female Dormitory: Shared dormitory room exclusively for female guests with bunk beds and shared bathrooms.

Good to Know:

- The Luna Hostel offers a relaxed and friendly environment, perfect for solo travelers or those looking to meet fellow adventurers.
- The hostel is located in a lively neighborhood, close to local attractions, markets, and dining options.
- Communal areas provide opportunities for guests to connect, share stories, and make new friends.
- The hostel staff are knowledgeable about the local area and can offer recommendations on nearby activities and sights.
- Basic amenities and facilities are provided to ensure a comfortable and convenient stay.

The Luna Hostel is an affordable and sociable choice for travelers seeking a cozy and welcoming atmosphere in Phuket. With its budget-friendly accommodations, communal spaces, and friendly staff, it offers a relaxed and enjoyable stay for those exploring the area on a limited budget.

3. BearPacker Patong Hostel

BearPacker Patong Hostel is a vibrant and affordable hostel located in the lively Patong Beach area of Phuket, Thailand. With its welcoming atmosphere, comfortable accommodations, and convenient location, it offers budget-conscious travelers a delightful and social experience.

Property Amenities:

- Common lounge area with cozy seating and a communal atmosphere for socializing and meeting fellow travelers.
- Outdoor terrace or garden where guests can relax and soak up the tropical ambiance.
- Communal kitchen and dining area for guests to prepare their own meals and share culinary experiences.
- 24-hour front desk service with friendly staff available to assist with inquiries and recommendations.
- Free Wi-Fi access available throughout the property.
- Laundry facilities for guests' convenience.
- Tour desk to help guests arrange excursions, activities, and transportation.

Room Features:

- Comfortable bunk beds with individual reading lights, privacy curtains, and personal lockers.
- Air conditioning or fans in the rooms for a comfortable stay.
- Shared bathrooms with hot showers and complimentary toiletries.
- Power outlets and USB charging ports near each bed.
- Bed linens and towels provided for guests.

Room Types:

- Mixed Dormitory: Shared dormitory room with bunk beds and shared bathrooms.
- Female Dormitory: Shared dormitory room exclusively for female guests with bunk beds and shared bathrooms.

Good to Know:

- BearPacker Patong Hostel offers a friendly and sociable environment, ideal for solo travelers or those looking to meet fellow adventurers.
- The hostel is located in the vibrant Patong Beach area, close to the beach, nightlife, and local attractions.

- Communal areas provide opportunities for guests to connect, share stories, and make new friends.
- The hostel staff are knowledgeable about the local area and can offer recommendations on nearby activities and sights.
- Basic amenities and facilities are provided to ensure a comfortable and convenient stay.

BearPacker Patong Hostel is a budget-friendly choice for travelers seeking a lively and social atmosphere in Patong Beach. With its affordable accommodations, communal spaces, and friendly staff, it offers a relaxed and enjoyable stay for those exploring Phuket on a limited budget.

Top homestays in Phuket

1. Phuket Gay Homestay - Neramit Hill

Phuket Gay Homestay - Neramit Hill is a welcoming and inclusive accommodation option situated in Phuket, Thailand. Designed specifically for LGBTQ+ travelers, it offers a safe and comfortable environment where guests can feel at home and connect with like-minded individuals.

Property Amenities:

- Cozy communal areas where guests can socialize, relax, and meet fellow LGBTQ+ travelers.
- Outdoor terrace or garden with tranquil surroundings for relaxation and enjoyment.
- Shared kitchen facilities for guests to prepare meals and interact with other guests.
- 24-hour front desk service with friendly staff available to assist with inquiries and recommendations.
- Free Wi-Fi access available throughout the property.
- Services for visitors' convenience, including laundry and dry cleaning.
- Tour desk to help guests arrange excursions, activities, and transportation.

Room Features:

- Comfortable and well-maintained rooms with a welcoming atmosphere.
- Choice of private or shared bathrooms, depending on room type.
- Air conditioning or fans in the rooms for a comfortable stay.
- Bed linens provided for guests.

Good to Know:

- Phuket Gay Homestay - Neramit Hill offers a safe and inclusive environment, catering specifically to LGBTQ+ travelers.
- The homestay is situated in a peaceful location, providing a respite from the bustling city while still being accessible to nearby attractions.
- Communal areas provide opportunities for guests to connect, share experiences, and create lasting friendships.
- The homestay staff are LGBTQ+ friendly and can provide recommendations on local LGBTQ+ hotspots, events, and attractions.
- Basic amenities and facilities are provided to ensure a comfortable and enjoyable stay.

Phuket Gay Homestay - Neramit Hill is a welcoming and inclusive option for LGBTQ+ travelers visiting Phuket. With its warm and accepting environment, communal spaces, and friendly staff, it provides a home away from home where guests can relax, connect, and enjoy their stay on this beautiful island.

2. Thai Siam Residence

Thai Siam Residence is a charming and tranquil accommodation nestled in the heart of Phuket, Thailand. With its authentic Thai architecture, warm hospitality, and peaceful surroundings, it offers a serene and comfortable stay for travelers seeking a traditional Thai experience.

Property Amenities:

- Lush garden area with beautiful flora and fauna, creating a serene and relaxing atmosphere.
- Outdoor swimming pool for guests to unwind and cool off.
- Delicious Thai and foreign food is served at the on-site restaurant.
- 24-hour front desk service with friendly staff available to assist with inquiries and recommendations.
- There is free WiFi accessible all across the place.
- Airport shuttle service for convenient transportation to and from the residence.

- Services for visitors' convenience, including laundry and dry cleaning.
- Tour desk to help guests arrange excursions, activities, and transportation.

Room Features:

- Thoughtfully designed and spacious rooms with traditional Thai decor and furnishings.
- Private balconies or terraces offering views of the surrounding gardens or pool area.
- Air conditioning for a comfortable stay in the tropical climate.
- entertainment options include flat-screen TVs with cable..
- Mini-bar, coffee/tea making facilities, and in-room dining options for added convenience.
- En-suite bathrooms with showers, complimentary toiletries, and hairdryers.

Good to Know:

- Thai Siam Residence provides an authentic Thai experience with its traditional architecture and warm hospitality.
- The residence is located in a peaceful area, allowing guests to relax and rejuvenate.

- The on-site restaurant offers a delightful selection of Thai and international dishes to tantalize the taste buds.
- The friendly staff are knowledgeable about the local area and can provide recommendations on nearby attractions and activities.
- Basic amenities and facilities are provided to ensure a comfortable and convenient stay.

Thai Siam Residence offers a serene and authentic Thai retreat in the heart of Phuket. With its traditional architecture, tranquil surroundings, and warm hospitality, it provides a peaceful and memorable stay for travelers seeking an immersive Thai experience.

3. Ice Kamala Beach Hotel

Ice Kamala Beach Hotel is a contemporary and stylish hotel situated in Kamala Beach, Phuket. With its sleek design, modern amenities, and prime beachfront location, it offers a luxurious and unforgettable experience for guests seeking a beach getaway.

Property Amenities:

- Direct access to Kamala Beach, allowing guests to enjoy the sun, sand, and sea.
- Rooftop swimming pool with panoramic views of the Andaman Sea.

- On-site restaurant offering a range of international and Thai cuisine.
- Fitness center equipped with state-of-the-art exercise equipment.
- 24-hour front desk service with attentive staff available to assist with inquiries and recommendations.
- Complimentary Wi-Fi access available throughout the property.
- Airport shuttle service for convenient transportation to and from the hotel.
- Services for visitors' convenience, including laundry and dry cleaning.
- Tour desk to help guests arrange excursions, activities, and transportation.

Room Features:

- Stylishly designed rooms with contemporary furnishings and a soothing color palette.
- Private balconies offering views of the beach or surrounding area.
- Comfortable beds with premium bedding for a restful sleep.
- Air conditioning and soundproofing for a peaceful and comfortable stay.

- entertainment options include flat-screen TVs with cable.
- Mini-bar, coffee/tea making facilities, and in-room dining options for added convenience.
- En-suite bathrooms with showers, complimentary toiletries, and hairdryers.
- Work desk and seating area for business travelers or those needing a dedicated workspace.

Good to Know:

- Ice Kamala Beach Hotel boasts a prime beachfront location, allowing guests to enjoy the beauty of Kamala Beach.
- The rooftop pool offers a relaxing spot to unwind and soak up the stunning views.
- The hotel's restaurant serves delectable dishes, providing a delightful culinary experience.
- The attentive staff are available to provide recommendations on nearby attractions, dining options, and activities.
- Basic amenities and facilities are provided to ensure a comfortable and convenient stay.

Ice Kamala Beach Hotel offers a modern and luxurious retreat in Kamala Beach. With its prime beachfront location, stylish rooms, and excellent amenities, it is an ideal choice for travelers seeking a beachside oasis in Phuket.

8.3 Dining and Cuisine

8.3 Dining and Cuisine: Phuket is a food lover's paradise, offering a diverse culinary scene that caters to all tastes and preferences. Here's what you can expect when it comes to dining and cuisine in Phuket.

- Thai Cuisine: Indulge in authentic Thai cuisine that tantalizes your taste buds with its vibrant flavors and aromatic spices. From Pad Thai and Green Curry to Tom Yum Soup and Mango Sticky Rice, the local Thai dishes are a must-try. Visit local restaurants, street food stalls, or upscale dining establishments to savor the best of Thai cuisine.
- Seafood: Being an island, Phuket is renowned for its fresh and delicious seafood. You'll find an abundance of seafood restaurants offering an array of dishes, from grilled fish and prawns to seafood curries and stir-fried delights. Head to beachfront areas like Rawai or Patong to enjoy a seafood feast.
- International Cuisine: Phuket also caters to international palates, with a wide range of international restaurants serving cuisines from around the world. Whether you're craving Italian pizza, Japanese sushi, Indian curry, or American burgers, you'll find an extensive selection of international eateries throughout the island.

- Street Food: Phuket's street food scene is a delight for food enthusiasts. Explore local markets and street stalls to sample a variety of dishes like Phad Thai, satay skewers, grilled seafood, fresh fruit shakes, and more. Not only is street food delicious, but it also offers an authentic and affordable dining experience.
- Fine Dining: If you're looking for a refined and upscale dining experience, Phuket has a range of fine dining establishments. These restaurants often feature elegant settings, gourmet cuisine, and impeccable service. Enjoy a romantic dinner with ocean views or indulge in a multi-course tasting menu prepared by renowned chefs.

Additionally, Phuket is known for its vibrant nightlife scene, with numerous bars, clubs, and beach clubs offering a combination of drinks, entertainment, and dining. Some beach clubs even feature live music or DJ performances, adding to the lively atmosphere.

Whether you choose to savor Thai delicacies, feast on seafood, explore international flavors, or immerse yourself in the street food culture, Phuket promises a gastronomic adventure that will satisfy even the most discerning palates.

8.4 Money and Currency Exchange

8.4 Money and Currency Exchange: When visiting Phuket, it's important to have a basic understanding of the local currency and options for currency exchange. Here's what you need to know:

Thailand's national currency is the Thai Baht (THB). It is recommended to carry some cash in baht for small purchases and transactions.

- Currency Exchange: Currency exchange services are widely available in Phuket, including at airports, banks, exchange booths, and authorized money changers. It's advisable to compare exchange rates and fees before making a transaction. Be cautious when exchanging money with street vendors or unauthorized outlets to avoid scams or counterfeit currency.
- ATMs: ATMs are easily accessible throughout Phuket, allowing you to withdraw cash in Thai baht. Hotels, restaurants, and bigger institutions accept major credit cards. However, smaller local vendors may prefer cash transactions.
- Credit Cards: Credit cards such as Visa, MasterCard, and American Express are commonly accepted in Phuket, especially in larger establishments. It's always a good idea to carry some cash for places that may not accept cards or in case of any technical issues.
- Traveler's Checks: Traveler's checks are not widely used or accepted in Phuket. It's best to rely on cash or credit cards for your financial needs.

Tipping is not required in Thailand, however it is appreciated for excellent service. Some restaurants may include a service charge, but if not, leaving a small tip is customary, typically rounding up the bill or leaving a 10% tip.

8.5 Safety Tips and Emergency Contacts

8.5 Safety Tips and Emergency Contacts: Phuket is generally a safe destination for travelers, but it's always wise to take precautions and be aware of your surroundings. Here are some safety recommendations and emergency contact numbers to remember:

- Personal Safety: Take basic safety precautions such as keeping your valuables secure, using reputable transportation services, and avoiding isolated or poorly lit areas at night. Be cautious of pickpockets in crowded areas and keep an eye on your belongings.
- Water Safety: When swimming or engaging in water activities, pay attention to safety flags and follow instructions from lifeguards. Be aware of strong currents or dangerous tides, particularly during the monsoon season. Consider using a life jacket if you are not a good swimmer. Consider using a life jacket if you are not a good swimmer.
- Scams: Be cautious of common tourist scams, such as overpriced tours, gem scams, or tuk-tuk drivers offering excessive fares. Use authorized and

- reputable tour operators and negotiate prices in advance.
- Health and Medical Care: Ensure you have travel insurance that covers medical expenses. Phuket has several hospitals and clinics that provide quality healthcare services. It's advisable to carry necessary medications and take precautions against mosquito bites, especially in areas where mosquito borne diseases like dengue fever are prevalent.

Emergency Contacts:

- Tourist Police: 1155
- Police: 191
- Ambulance: 1669
- Fire: 199

It's always a good idea to stay updated on local news and follow any travel advisories or guidelines issued by your home country's government or embassy. By being mindful and taking necessary precautions, you can have a safe and enjoyable experience in Phuket.

Chalong temple at phuket

CHAPTER 9: OFF THE BEATEN PATH

9.1 Secret Beaches and Hidden Coves

9.1 Secret Beaches and Hidden Coves: While Phuket is known for its popular beaches, there are also some hidden gems that offer a more secluded and tranquil experience. Here are a few off-the-beaten-path beaches and hidden coves to explore:

- Ao Sane Beach: Tucked away between Nai Harn and Ya Nui beaches, Ao Sane Beach is a hidden paradise that remains relatively untouched by crowds. It features crystal-clear waters, vibrant coral reefs, and a serene atmosphere, perfect for snorkeling and sunbathing.
- Laem Singh Beach: Located between Kamala and Surin beaches, Laem Singh Beach is accessible only by boat or a steep staircase. This secluded cove offers soft white sand, turquoise waters, and a peaceful environment. It's an ideal spot for sunbathing, swimming, and picnicking.
- Yanui Beach: Nestled in the southern part of Phuket near Promthep Cape, Yanui Beach is a small and lesser-known beach. It boasts stunning views of the Andaman Sea, picturesque rock formations, and calm waters, making it a great spot for snorkeling and relaxing.

- Banana Beach: Situated on the northwest coast of Phuket, Banana Beach is a hidden gem accessible only by boat or a short hike through the jungle. This secluded beach offers privacy, soft sand, and turquoise waters. Swimming, snorkeling, and sunbathing are all ideal there.
- Freedom Beach: Located near Patong Beach, Freedom Beach is a secluded stretch of pristine sand accessible by boat or a hiking trail. Surrounded by lush vegetation, it offers a tranquil atmosphere, clear waters, and excellent snorkeling opportunities.

To explore these secret beaches and hidden coves, consider hiring a long-tail boat or joining a guided tour that specializes in off-the-beaten-path destinations. Keep in mind that some of these beaches may have limited facilities, so it's advisable to bring your own essentials such as food, water, and sun protection.

Discovering these hidden gems allows you to escape the crowds and experience the natural beauty of Phuket in a more intimate setting. Just remember to respect the environment, leave no trace, and adhere to any local regulations to preserve the pristine nature of these off-the-beaten-path locations.

9.2 Authentic Local Experiences

9.2 Authentic Local Experiences: To truly immerse yourself in the local culture of Phuket, consider engaging in authentic experiences that showcase the island's traditions and way of life. Here are some suggestions:

- Visit a Local Market: Explore the vibrant local markets, such as the Phuket Weekend Market or Banzaan Fresh Market, where you can browse through stalls selling fresh produce, local handicrafts, and delicious street food. Interact with friendly vendors and experience the lively atmosphere of a traditional Thai market.
- Take a Thai Cooking Class: Learn the art of Thai cuisine by joining a cooking class. Visit a local market to select fresh ingredients and then learn to prepare popular Thai dishes under the guidance of experienced chefs. It's a hands-on experience that allows you to savor the flavors of Thailand long after your trip.
- Witness a Traditional Thai Dance Performance: Attend a traditional Thai dance performance, such as the Ram Thai or Fawn Thai, which showcase the grace and beauty of Thai culture. These performances often include elaborate costumes, intricate movements, and enchanting music, providing a glimpse into the country's rich cultural heritage.
- Explore Old Phuket Town: Wander through the charming streets of Old Phuket Town and admire the well-preserved Sino-Portuguese architecture. Visit the local temples, browse art galleries and

boutiques, and dine at authentic Thai restaurants tucked away in this historic part of the island.

9.3 Day Trips from Phuket

9.3 Day Trips from Phuket: Phuket's strategic location offers the opportunity to embark on exciting day trips to nearby destinations. Here are some popular options:

- Phi Phi Islands: Explore the stunning Phi Phi Islands, known for their turquoise waters, limestone cliffs, and vibrant marine life. Take a boat tour to Maya Bay, snorkel in Pileh Lagoon, and enjoy the breathtaking beauty of this island paradise.
- Phang Nga Bay: Discover the iconic limestone karsts and emerald waters of Phang Nga Bay. Explore the famous James Bond Island (Koh Tapu), go sea kayaking through the mangroves, and visit the floating village of Koh Panyee.
- Similan Islands: Embark on a day trip to the Similan Islands, a group of picturesque islands renowned for their crystal-clear waters and coral reefs. Snorkel or dive in vibrant underwater ecosystems, relax on pristine beaches, and soak in the natural beauty of this national park.
- Krabi: Venture beyond Phuket and visit the nearby province of Krabi. Explore the stunning Railay Beach, go rock climbing on limestone cliffs, and take a boat tour to the breathtaking Phi Phi Islands or the picturesque Four Islands.

- Phuket Elephant Sanctuary: Support ethical elephant tourism by visiting the Phuket Elephant Sanctuary. This sanctuary provides a safe haven for rescued elephants, allowing you to observe these majestic creatures in a responsible and humane environment.

9.4 Eco-Tourism and Sustainable Initiatives

9.4 Eco-Tourism and Sustainable Initiatives: Phuket is increasingly focusing on eco-tourism and sustainable initiatives to preserve its natural beauty and protect the environment. Consider engaging in eco-friendly activities and supporting organizations that promote sustainability. Some options include:

- Snorkeling and Diving: Choose eco-friendly operators that prioritize reef conservation and follow responsible diving practices. Avoid stepping on or touching coral reefs and marine life, and be mindful of your impact on underwater ecosystems.
- Nature Reserves and Wildlife Sanctuaries: Visit nature reserves and wildlife sanctuaries like Sirinat National Park or Khao Phra Thaeo Wildlife Sanctuary. These protected areas allow you to observe local flora and fauna while supporting conservation efforts.
- Beach Cleanup Activities: Participate in beach cleanup initiatives organized by local NGOs or dive centers. Help keep the beaches clean by collecting

trash and raising awareness about the importance of maintaining a pristine coastline.
- Sustainable Accommodation: Choose eco-friendly accommodations that implement sustainable practices such as energy conservation, waste management, and support for local communities.
- Responsible Wildlife Interactions: When engaging in wildlife encounters, such as visiting elephant sanctuaries or wildlife rehabilitation centers, prioritize ethical establishments that prioritize the well-being and conservation of animals.

9.5 Exploring Nearby Islands and National Parks

9.5 Exploring Nearby Islands and National Parks: Phuket serves as a gateway to several stunning islands and national parks in the Andaman Sea region. Here are a few recommendations for exploration:

- Similan Islands: Known for their remarkable underwater biodiversity, the Similan Islands are a diver's paradise. Explore vibrant coral reefs, encounter exotic marine species, and enjoy the pristine beaches and lush landscapes.
- Khao Sok National Park: Venture inland to Khao Sok National Park, a verdant rainforest with towering limestone mountains, emerald lakes, and diverse

- wildlife. Go on jungle treks, kayak through scenic rivers, and discover the park's natural wonders.
- Racha Islands: Escape to the Racha Islands, located just a short boat ride from Phuket. These serene islands offer crystal-clear waters, vibrant coral reefs, and picturesque beaches. Snorkel, swim, or simply relax in this idyllic tropical paradise.
- Koh Yao Islands: Experience the tranquil and laid-back atmosphere of the Koh Yao Islands. These islands offer pristine beaches, lush mangrove forests, and a glimpse into the local way of life. Enjoy kayaking, cycling, or simply unwinding in this peaceful setting.
- Ao Phang Nga National Park: Explore the dramatic limestone karsts and emerald-green waters of Ao Phang Nga National Park. Take a boat tour through the maze-like mangrove forests, visit iconic islands, and marvel at the unique natural scenery.

When planning day trips or excursions, consider booking through reputable tour operators or local guides who prioritize sustainability and responsible tourism practices. This way, you can explore the beauty of Phuket's neighboring islands and national parks while minimizing your impact on the environment.

CHAPTER 10: CONCLUSION

10.1 Phuket: Your Unforgettable Experience

10.1 Phuket: Your Unforgettable Experience: Phuket, with its stunning beaches, rich cultural heritage, and vibrant atmosphere, offers a truly unforgettable experience for travelers. From exploring the historical charm of Old Phuket Town to indulging in the mouthwatering local cuisine, there is something for everyone on this tropical island. Whether you're seeking relaxation, adventure, or a mix of both, Phuket has it all.

Immerse yourself in the local culture by visiting temples and participating in traditional festivals. Dive into the turquoise waters and discover the diverse marine life through snorkeling and scuba diving. Embark on off-the-beaten-path adventures to secret beaches and hidden coves, or venture to nearby islands and national parks for breathtaking natural wonders.

As you explore Phuket, make sure to engage in sustainable and responsible tourism practices. Support eco-friendly initiatives, choose ethical wildlife interactions, and be mindful of your impact on the environment. By doing so, you can contribute to the preservation of Phuket's natural beauty for future generations to enjoy.

10.2 Travel Resources and Additional Information

10.2 Travel Resources and Additional Information: To enhance your Phuket travel experience, here are some helpful travel resources and additional information:

- Official Tourism Website: Visit the official website of the Tourism Authority of Thailand for comprehensive information on Phuket, including attractions, accommodations, and upcoming events.
- Online Travel Forums: Join online travel forums and communities to connect with fellow travelers, seek advice, and gather insider tips on the best places to visit in Phuket.
- Local Tour Operators: Engage the services of reputable local tour operators for guided tours, island hopping excursions, and adventure activities. They can provide valuable knowledge and ensure you have a safe and enjoyable experience.
- Local Transportation: Familiarize yourself with local transportation options such as taxis, tuk-tuks, songthaews (shared minibusses), and motorbike rentals. Be aware of standard fares or negotiate prices in advance.
- Travel Insurance: Prioritize travel insurance that covers medical emergencies, trip cancellations, and personal belongings. Ensure it offers comprehensive coverage for your specific travel needs.

- Local Customs and Etiquette: Respect the local customs and traditions of Thailand, such as removing your shoes before entering temples or dressing modestly when visiting religious sites.
- Weather Updates: Stay informed about weather conditions in Phuket, especially during the monsoon season (May to October), to plan your activities accordingly.
- Health and Safety: Check the latest travel advisories, follow health and safety guidelines, and consult your healthcare provider regarding any necessary vaccinations or precautions before traveling to Phuket.

By utilizing these travel resources and seeking additional information, you can make the most of your trip to Phuket and ensure a smooth and memorable experience.

As you embark on your Phuket adventure, remember to embrace the beauty of the island, engage with the local culture, and create lifelong memories. Enjoy the breathtaking beaches, indulge in delicious cuisine, and take in the warm hospitality of the Thai people. Phuket awaits you with its enchanting allure, ready to provide an unforgettable travel experience in the year 2023 and beyond.

Printed in Great Britain
by Amazon